THE
ENNEAGRAM
TYPE 3
journal

A Guide to Inner Work & Self-Discovery
for The Achiever

THIS JOURNAL BELONGS TO:

Published in the United States by: Hay House LLC: www.hayhouse.com®
Published in Australia by: Hay House Australia Pty. Ltd.: www.hayhouse.com.au
Published in the United Kingdom by: Hay House UK, Ltd.: www.hayhouse.co.uk
Published in India by: Hay House Publishers India: www.hayhouse.co.in

Cover design: Julie Davison
Interior design: Lisi Mohandessi
Author photo: Courtesy of Deborah Threadgill Egerton, Ph.D.

Tradepaper ISBN: 978-1-4019-7903-4
10 9 8 7 6 5 4 3 2 1
1st edition, May 2024

This product uses responsibly sourced papers and/or recycled materials. For more information, see www.hayhouse.com.

Printed and bound by CPI Group (UK) Ltd, Croydon, CR0 4YY

MIX
Paper | Supporting
responsible forestry
FSC® C013604

THE
ENNEAGRAM
TYPE 3
journal

DEBORAH THREADGILL EGERTON, Ph.D.
& LISI MOHANDESSI

HAY HOUSE LLC
Carlsbad, California • New York City
London • Sydney • New Delhi

This journal is dedicated to
Julie Forker,
who turned ordinary moments
into extraordinary memories.

You are gifted with a body that allows you to be here in the present moment, a mind that opens access to unlimited possibilities to be explored, and a heart that holds the enormous capacity to love and be loved.

This is the authentic you. You will find yourself when you accept the beauty of your true nature.

Gratitude for who you are is the first step.

Grace will follow.

Caritas,
Deborah & Lisi

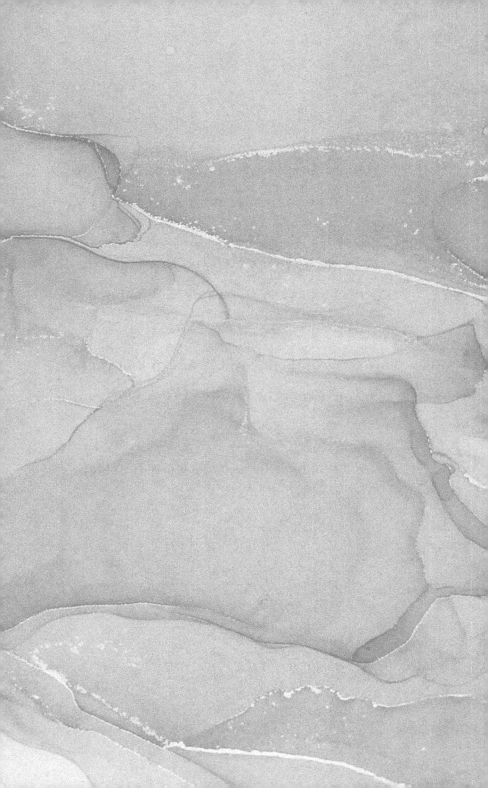

CONTENTS

*Enjoy your journey, and
may you find love and
light within yourself.*

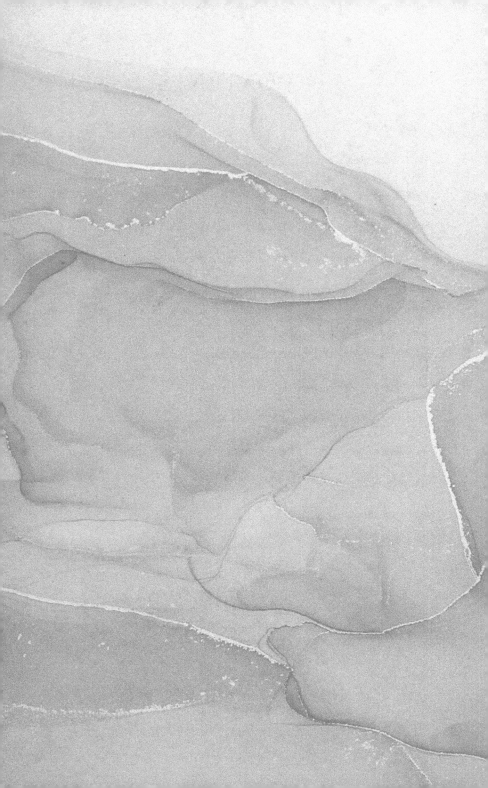

INTRODUCTION

Many of us journey through life pondering the reasons behind our actions and how we can enrich our lives. We seek not only improvement but also a sense of tranquility, productivity, and purpose. Conversations with friends, colleagues, mentors, and partners often echo the advice to "do the work." This phrase never fails to elicit a knowing smile because if it were that simple, we would already be immersed in the process of "doing the work." Yet we continually find ourselves returning to the fundamental question: What is the work?

A deep understanding of oneself is necessary to live a life brimming with abundance, creativity, joy, and love. Self-awareness is a journey inward, a voyage to explore how we present ourselves to the world, and the Enneagram will serve as our guide. Clues about our true selves are sometimes scattered before us, but we often choose to look away from anything that challenges our self-image. This is why the voyage inward, toward self-realization, becomes indispensable in uncovering our genuine, authentic selves.

This journal is thoughtfully crafted to accompany you on this very journey as you harness the insights of the Enneagram. Within these pages you'll encounter an array of writing prompts, mindfulness exercises, inspirational quotes, and grounding meditations for introspection. Each page is a deliberate step along your unique path. It's crucial to remember that this process cannot be hurried or coerced. Guidance on this voyage comes from a source known by many names—God, the Universe, the Divine, Spirit, or a name entirely personal to your experience. All these concepts are interconnected. You need not adhere to any dogmatic religious structure; what truly matters is connecting with that part of you that acknowledges a higher force, shaping and influencing your choices and your path forward.

This journal isn't something you casually dip into; rather, it's an invitation to cultivate a consistent habit of exploring its pages, allowing you to fully embrace the practices within. These pages are designed to guide you toward a profound understanding of why you do what you do.

The Enneagram stands out as a radiant gem among the many personality typing systems, and it beckons with a warm, unique approach centered on uncovering motivations rather than mere behaviors. It opens a doorway to explore the why behind our actions, inviting us to discover the roots of our behaviors. As we delve into this exploration, we find newfound flexibility, unlocking exciting possibilities we may have never imagined before.

We encourage you to delve deeper into the understanding of your dominant Enneagram energy, which is akin to picking up a mirror to gaze upon yourself in a way you've never done before. The idea may initially seem a bit intimidating, but the richness of your life is directly linked to the depth you're willing to explore within your soul.

Your life inherently possesses meaning, purpose, and a trajectory leading toward goodness; it's our natural inclination. Sometimes, we find ourselves needing to reconnect with what truly matters. We might start to wonder and feel disoriented when we sense that we've drifted away from our guiding light. But remember, that guidance hasn't abandoned us; it's possible we've simply strayed from it, unable to see what's right in front of us.

As you embark on this journey, we wish you all the goodness and benefits it has to offer. It's not about reaching a final destination but about following your guiding light, aligning yourself with what's genuine, trustworthy, and good in both the world and within yourself. Return to the pages of this journal daily, allowing your journey to inform you and lead you toward truth, joy, love, light, and goodness. All these elements reside within you, and they'll never abandon you. Sources of love and joy perpetually surround us, and by embracing the truth of goodness in the world, you'll radiate with the light found inside yourself.

This journal is designed as your reference guide and exploratory workbook. The following section will gently guide you through the Enneagram system and provide an overview of Type Three energy. Within these pages, you'll find a wealth of knowledge about the Enneagram; and using this journal is a chance to reignite your inner connection with your Enneagram Three energy. Prepare yourself, for your mind will be engaged, your heart will be touched, and your body will respond; all of these experiences, both uplifting and challenging, are an integral part of the journey. We hope you continue to revisit these pages as you further your journey deeper into the Enneagram system.

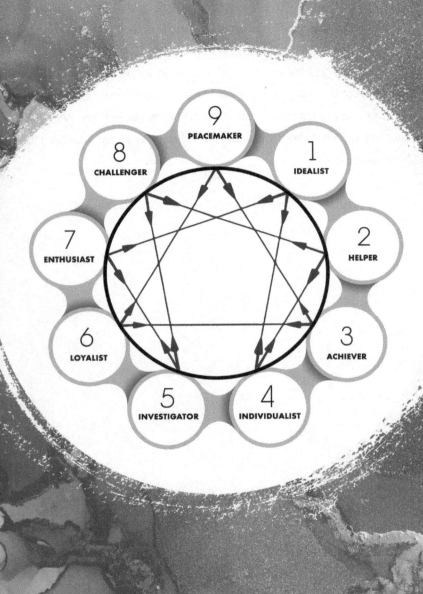

The Enneagram

The Enneagram is an archetypal personality system that combines modern psychological practices with a deep foundation in ancient traditions, religions, cultures, and spiritual practices. It is a model of the human psyche taught as a typology of nine personality archetypes. These types have names that reflect the nine different energies: Eight, Challenger; Nine, Peacemaker; One, Idealist; Two, Helper; Three, Achiever; Four, Individualist; Five, Investigator; Six, Loyalist; and Seven, Enthusiast.

The Enneagram invites you to embark on a journey of self-discovery, unlocking the intricate mechanisms governing your existence. It allows you to delve into the why behind your actions and the how of your daily functioning in pursuit of fulfilling your needs. Unveiling your core motivations, values, fears, and inherent strengths is a perpetual source of insight. Simultaneously, the Enneagram casts light on the egoic patterns that occasionally hinder our progress, thwarting our alignment with our true selves. More significantly, while this insightful system aids us in uncovering our authentic selves, it equally guides us in connecting with others, fostering appreciation, and cultivating genuine presence.

This beginning section is designed to serve as a refresher on the basics of the Enneagram and a quick look into each of the nine types. Remember: the Enneagram is a fluid system that provides access to all nine types, and we encourage you to explore your relationship with all of these energies.

The moment you intentionally chose to use this journal, you began your journey to discover who you really are instead of creating another version of yourself. Or, as people like to say, "the best version of yourself." Your goal now is to find out who you are underneath all the versions of yourself that you have created. Welcome to the journey of your lifetime! May you find joy, peace, acceptance, and belonging in this exploration. May love be your path, and may light shine on every step you take. Most importantly, may you fall deeply in love with the authentic you. The glorious being that you were created to be.

A QUICK OVERVIEW OF THE BASICS OF THE ENNEAGRAM

TYPE/POINT

Each of the nine Enneagram points possesses unique energies and characteristics. When discussing an Enneagram type, we are identifying the specific point on the Enneagram where one embodies the most significant energy. It's important to note that we have access to all nine points on the Enneagram, each contributing to our holistic understanding and personal growth.

CENTERS OF INTELLIGENCE

The Enneagram is explored through three Centers of Intelligence: Body, Heart, and Head. Sometimes, these centers, or triads, are called Body/Instinctive, Heart/Feeling, and Head/Thinking. Each center has a connection to particular emotions: the Body, anger and rage (Eight, Nine, One); the Heart, shame and guilt (Two, Three, Four); and the Head, fear and anxiety (Five, Six, Seven).

BASIC DESIRE AND BASIC FEAR

We all have inner drive and internalized fear that affect all of our behaviors, beliefs, and actions. You may resonate with all nine basic fears and desires, as we are beings composed of all nine energies; however, you will have the most substantial connection to one corresponding fear and desire of one specific type.

CORE MOTIVATION

The core motivation constantly challenges us to get what we most desire at any given moment while avoiding what we fear that will cause our demise. The core motivation is your internal drive, the reason you wake up in the morning, how you navigate life, and that thing that gets you going or paralyzes you. Think of the core motivation as why you do what you do.

WINGS

The types on either side of your dominant Enneagram energy affect how your type shows up in the world. Every Enneagram type has two wings; however, one of the wings may significantly influence the energy of your dominant Enneagram type.

LINES AND ARROWS

The Enneagram lines and arrows, also referred to as the stress and security points or directions of growth and stress, connect the types across the map. There are multiple ways of using the lines and arrows when we see them as connections to pick up specific qualities at specific times. We can move freely between these connections, picking up positive and negative energies as we need them to create a warning system and a path for growth.

PASSION: THE WAY WE SUFFER—PERSONAL CHALLENGE

The passions represent the nine main ways we lose our center, become more susceptible to personality distortions, and become disoriented from reality. We can refer to each of the passions as the way in which each type suffers.

FIXATION: HOW WE GET STUCK—THE TRAP

We all have a way of becoming trapped in our personality, which we see play out through the fixation. These "traps" are mental blocks we hold on to when attempting to justify our reality.

VIRTUE: OUR TRUE NATURE—THE GIFT

Honoring our true selves and who we become develops when we land in our virtue. These specific characteristics manifest through the emotional awareness of the authentic self, and the letting go of ego, self-deception, and dynamic vices. When we access our virtue, we become selfless and altruistic in our actions, feelings, and beliefs.

INSTINCTS

The Instincts, sometimes referred to as Subtypes and Instinctual Variants, within each Enneagram energy are Self-Preservation, Social, and Sexual (sometimes referred to as One-on-One). The Instincts can be mirrored in the three drives for survival: preserving life and focusing on physical needs, mutual cooperation and creating social bonds, and species survival through exploration and experiencing energies. We have a dominant instinct that we feel most comfortable with and a secondary instinct to support the dominant one. The third instinct is usually the least developed, therefore, an area that manifests as an unseen personal challenge.

LEVELS OF DEVELOPMENT

The Levels of Development established by Don Riso and Russ Hudson demonstrate the varying degrees of how each type can show up in the world based on presence. Healthy, average, and unhealthy refer to the Levels of Development and the overall state of a person's ability to function. The energy of each type can show up very differently depending on how healthy or unhealthy the individual is; this is a common reason why many people mistype or feel uncomfortable as their dominant type.

Healthy—Becoming expansive and unconstricted in essence, fully present in the world

Average—Beginning to allow our egos to guide our behaviors, dropping into destructive patterns when we fall asleep to our true selves, with a fluctuation of presence

Unhealthy—Dysfunctional and destructive behaviors when ego becomes the driving force behind everything we do; falling into ego-based patterns that trap us in personality

HEALTHY	L1	BEING	Freedom from Ego Structure
	L2	ALLOWING	Psychological Capacity ("I Am")
	L3	DOING	Social Value / Gift
AVERAGE	L4	EFFORTING	Social Role / Imbalance
	L5	IMPOSING	Interpersonal Control
	L6	AGGRESSION	Overcompensation
UNHEALTHY	L7	VIOLATING	Violation
	L8	COMPULSIVE	Delusion & Compulsion
	L9	DESTROYING	Pathological Destruction

ADAPTED FROM THE RISO-HUDSON LEVELS OF DEVELOPMENT

8

THINGS TO REMEMBER

- There are nine points on the Enneagram map. We can access all the points but lead with one dominant type. The numbers are not a scale, meaning no type is better or worse than any other type. However, in order to keep the Enneagram energies grouped by the centers of intelligence, we look at the types in this order: Eight, Nine, One, Two, Three, Four, Five, Six, Seven.

- Your dominant Enneagram type does not change throughout your life or shift based on your home or work life. You are born into your type, and your experiences adjust how you navigate life, access your wing energy, travel with the arrows, and drop into the Levels of Development.

- No type is inherently gendered or dependent on dimensions of diversity (perceived race, socioeconomic status, education, age, religion, etc.). While the descriptions and energies of the types are universal and are not dependent on certain identifying factors, it is essential to note how an Enneagram energy can vary based on cultural or environmental influences or psychological well-being. For instance, some cultures have specific gender roles, socially acceptable values, or religious influences that can impact the Enneagram energy. Still, these factors do not fundamentally change a person's dominant Enneagram type.

- No one can tell you where you stand on the Enneagram map. You find your place by reading about and exploring all aspects of the nine types. Tests can help you narrow down the choices, and you may find your type by process of elimination. Tests are not always the defining factor of where you stand on the Enneagram map; the tests' quality matters.

KEY DESCRIPTORS OF
THE NINE TYPES

The descriptors for each Enneagram type listed below begin on the high side of the energy and transition into the low side of the energy.

THE BODY CENTER

8 self-confident, authoritative, hardworking, strong-willed, forceful, passionate, outspoken, independent, protective, abundant energy, maintaining power and control, defensive, combative, "invulnerable," harsh, rageful, vengeful, boastful, demonstrative, tyrannical, omnipotent

9 receptive, reassuring, agreeable, considerate, quiet, easygoing, thoughtful, accepting, supportive, accommodating, dependable, stable, hardworking, pragmatic, complacent, disengaged, emotionally indolent, indifferent, angry, stubborn, dissociated, numb, apathetic

1 principled, purposeful, organized, ethical, fastidious, fair, objective, sense of mission, practical action, high standards, inner critic, highly critical, impatient, repressed, angry, controlling, perfectionistic, puritanical, resentful, emotionally constricted, scolding, abrasive, punitive, inflexible

THE HEART CENTER

2 generous, empathetic, helpful, thoughtful, caring, reliable, compassionate, kind, overly considerate, people-pleasing, seductive, intrusive, possessive, seeking validation, angry, resentful, hurt, manipulative, flattering, demonstrative, low self-esteem/value

3 hardworking, dedicated, driven, ambitious, resourceful, impressive, motivated, highly skilled, distinguished, pragmatic, opportunistic, calculating, narcissistic, impostor syndrome, seeking validation and attention, social climber, arrogant, unprincipled, self-centered, conceited

4 emotional, empathetic, creative, unique, connected, deep, romantic, authentic, eccentric, poetic, introspective, sensitive, moody, manipulative, judgmental, self-conscious, tormented, dark, depressive, angry, lost, self-destructive, hopeless, despair, macabre, self-absorbed

THE HEAD CENTER

5 competent, capable, cerebral, wise, highly skilled, well-rounded, eccentric, pioneering, complex, perceptive, independent, inventive, visionary, secretive, withdrawn, antagonistic, cynical, argumentative, reclusive, intellectually arrogant, self-destructive, nihilistic, erratic

6 innovative, structured, hardworking, intensely loyal, reliable, security-oriented, troubleshooting, revolutionary, engaging, contradictory, dependent, indecisive, untrusting, defensive, reactive, fearful, insecure, stubborn, suspicious, erratic, worst-case scenario, panicked, paranoid

7 free-spirited, fun, happy, curious, joyful, optimistic, adventurous, fast learners, well-rounded, humorous, bold, vivacious, life of the party, flaky, self-centered, narcissistic, emotionally stunted, insensitive, impulsive, escapist mentality, erratic, compulsive, panic-stricken, avoidance, jaded

**Which descriptors from your Enneagram energy
do you resonate with the most and why?**

_____

_____

_____

_____

_____

_____

_____

_____

_____

_____

_____

_____

Enneagram Type Three

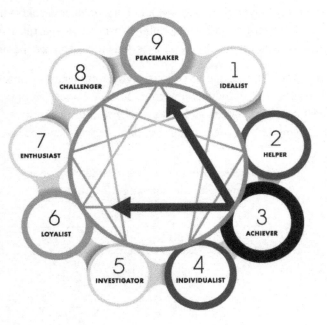

DESCRIPTORS FOR THREE ENERGY

driven, hardworking, ambitious, self-assured, successful,
achievement-oriented, charming, diplomatic, seeking
validation, image-conscious, competitive, ego-driven,
opportunistic, narcissistic, deceitful, manipulative,
impostor syndrome, shape-shifting, fear of failure

Basic Desire: to feel valuable, worthwhile, to be successful and admirable

Basic Fear: to be a failure, to feel worthless and of no value, to be unsuccessful, to feel deficient

Core Motivation: to be affirmed, to distinguish self from others, to have attention, to be admired and impress others, to appear worthy for what is accomplished in order to hide low self-worth / poor self-image

Passion/The Personal Challenge: Deceit—manifests as a constant drive to present yourself in a way that does not reflect the authentic self but instead creates a mask of value

Fixation/The Trap: Vanity—you seek out opportunities to prove own worth by manipulating the truth to serve own need to succeed and thus prove value

Virtue/The Gift: Truthfulness— acceptance of the authentic self in that you are loved not for what you do, but for who you are, you move out into the world with honesty and genuineness

Wings: Two and Four

Arrows: Six and Nine

Threes want to be:

- valuable and worthwhile
- affirmed and to excel
- effective and efficient
- able to perform in an impressive manner
- the best
- admired and able to garner praise and attention

Threes do not want to be:

- anything that looks like failure
- a person who sits around doing nothing
- overshadowed by others
- unprepared or awkward
- average
- forced to ask others for help or support
- caught in distortions of the truth

LEVELS OF DEVELOPMENT
AS A TYPE THREE

HEALTHY LEVELS OF DEVELOPMENT

As a Three operating in the healthy Levels of Development, you become self-accepting, authentic, modest, and charitable. You can use self-deprecatory humor to make people feel comfortable and at ease if they are intimidated by your truly impressive gifts. A fullness of heart emerges, and you are no longer afraid of dealing with true emotions as they arise. You become gentle and benevolent, leading with authenticity and inspirational charisma. You are willing to face failure with principled strength and resilience, leading with kindness and selflessness in the face of division, confrontation, and conflict. When healthy you have found truthfulness in the ability to access your authentic self and take right action with a collective awareness rather than a self-centered approach. You oftentimes will find worthy causes and channel your energy into making the cause successful and impactful, sometimes finding a supporting role without needing to be front and center. The need to project a "desirable" identity in order to maintain validation transforms into the emotional awareness for growth over progress.

AVERAGE LEVELS OF DEVELOPMENT

Most humans reside within these average levels and fluctuate up or down depending on the circumstances they find themselves in. As a Three drops down into the average Levels of Development, the ego agenda begins to take over. The fluctuations can create opportunities for you to pause and cultivate the presence needed to examine your thoughts and actions and course correct. This allows for you to move back up in the levels and avoid falling back into unhealthy patterns of behavior and thought. However, as the ability for self-reflection and course correction wanes, you can begin to project a fraudulent self-image; unwilling to engage authentically, you become shape-shifting, stubborn, self-absorbed, shameful, and apathetic toward other people. In some cases you can become conceited, self-serving, emotionally stunted, ultimately deflecting your authentic self and repressing your capacity for humility. You are apprehensive of forward progress or sacrifice without the guarantee of success; your apathy is caused by fear of failure. Often a deeply hurt or insecure individual who feels that you must be on top to be valued—never overshadowed or outdone by others—you become deceptive and dishonest, bending your truth to become whatever will make you the most "impressive." Your self-image becomes interwoven with how you are perceived by others and may not actually represent your authentic self. Impostor syndrome can become a recurring theme for you as you fluctuate within the average Levels of Development. The guilt and shame at these levels can morph into a combination of deceit, vanity, and low self-value and cause you to drop further down the levels. It takes a great deal of self-reflection and inner work to rise through the levels and avoid dropping further.

UNHEALTHY LEVELS OF DEVELOPMENT

When you drop into the unhealthy levels, you become extremely egotistical, self-centered, dishonest, vindictive, and duplicitous. You begin to justify your destructive actions and behaviors from the unhealthy energy of Type Three. You can also become relentless and obsessive about destroying whatever reminds you of your own shortcomings and failures. Fear, shame, and low self-worth are the primary motivators that distort your reality, resulting in a destructive arrogance that facilitates the dehumanization and dismissal of anyone who challenges your value. Deep down you fear that someone has seen through your facade and knows how much shame you are holding on to, which can trigger feelings of deep guilt and worthlessness. This only reinforces your aversion to failure, which will further fuel deceitful and narcissistic behaviors.

You can refer back to the Levels of Development to see where you are at any point in time. Make notes on your progress below:

_____

_____

_____

_____

_____

_____

WINGS

*Remember, you have access to both wings. Some people
identify strongly with one wing energy over the other, but
both wings still affect how your dominant type appears.*

THREE WITH A STRONG TWO WING

Dedicated, self-aware, efficient in making things happen, deep concern for
people, warm and caring, self-centered and focused on image, possessive
and unintentionally manipulative

THREE WITH A STRONG FOUR WING

Adaptable, connected to others, strive to improve yourself and others,
emotionally aware and receptive to others, overly competitive and
egotistical, manipulative and emotionally distorted, begin acting with
hidden agenda

ARROWS

*Remember, you have access to both arrows, and you can
move freely between these connections. This movement
allows you to pick up positive and negative energies as needed
and creates a warning system and a path for growth.*

THREE'S ARROW TO SIX

Deeply connected to finding solutions where you are instead of manipulating
situations, become self-absorbed, highly indecisive, anxiety and fear take
over, self-doubt and impostor syndrome

THREE'S ARROW TO NINE

Ability to pause for reflection and emotional honesty, grounded in the
moment to become present in order to grow, aimless and apathetic,
detached from compassion and self-awareness, overwhelmed and stressed

INSTINCTS

As balanced human beings, we naturally have all three instincts within us. However, we have a dominant instinct that we feel most comfortable with and a secondary instinct to support the dominant one. The third instinct is usually the least developed, therefore, an area that manifests as an unseen personal challenge.

SELF-PRESERVATION THREE

If you are a Self-Preservation Three, you are typically focused on working hard to ensure your security and stability. You tend to maximize your efforts in career growth and financial stability. You strive for success, recognition, and advancement in your career or social standing. You probably have a very hard time taking it easy, slowing down, or relaxing. You may neglect relationships and family obligations. You're detail-oriented and fastidious in different areas of your life, much like One energy, but you may not adhere to a moral compass and instead strive for achievement by any means necessary.

SOCIAL THREE

As a Social Three, you can focus much of your energy on your status as a way of establishing a clearly impressive role in your social circles. You may rely on recognition and reassurance that you are impressive. You may feel anxious to prove above and beyond that you are at the top of your group. You will not accept being second best or being outdone in any way, much like Two energy in terms of seeking validation and attention. You can feel the need to brag about yourself, name drop, or indulge in an exaggeration of your achievements and success.

SEXUAL THREE

If you identify with the Sexual instinct in Three, you may focus your energy on becoming the "human ideal." You enjoy being admired and will strive to be incredibly impressive, alluring, and desirable. You want to be desired, and you want other people to acknowledge that you are desirable. You will find partners and cultivate a small group of a few close friends. But unlike the Two, who focus their attention on the other people, the attention is drawn inward as you use your alluring qualities to bring people closer to you. While radiating a magnetic energy, you can also repel people as you begin to feel uncomfortable with your own emotions and deeply repressed shame.

THREE'S RESPONSES
TO CONFLICTS

UNHEALTHY REACTION

Vanity over advocacy, inability to speak up, narcissism, false sense of self-image, inaction, jealousy, avoidance, emotional distortion, shame, misdirected anger, distorting the truth to fulfill a deep-seated need to be seen as valuable, emotionally demonstrative displays aimed at people who challenge your identity of being a valuable/worthy/successful person

HEALTHY REACTION

Pause for honest reflection, courage, compassion, empathy, emotional honesty, externally focused, balanced self-awareness and communal aware-ness, outspoken and fierce challenges to biased, bigoted, and discriminatory situations, genuine desire to be present and honest with no hidden agenda, ability to take action, motivational charisma manifests and inspires others to get involved and show up with the same level of drive and ambition

Reflections on your experience of unhealthy and healthy responses:

_____

_____

_____

_____

_____

_____

_____

_____

_____

_____

EXAMPLES OF THREE ENERGY

Oprah Winfrey, Marianne Williamson, Brené Brown, Will Smith, Deepak Chopra, Bill Clinton, Jesse Jackson, Mitt Romney, Candace Owens, Tony Robbins, Beyoncé, Muhammed Ali, Meghan Markle, Michael Jordan, Tiger Woods, Lance Armstrong, Elvis Presley, Paul McCartney, Madonna, Sting, Whitney Houston, Jamie Foxx

Explore your connection to one or more of these people who demonstrate strong Three energy. What is it about their character or personality that reminds you most of yourself?

_____

_____

_____

_____

_____

_____

_____

_____

_____

_____

_____

_____

_____

_____

_____

How do you experience the different elements of Three energy within yourself?

_____

_____

_____

_____

_____

_____

_____

_____

_____

_____

_____

_____

_____

_____

_____

_____

_____

_____

_____

_____

_____

_____

_____

_____

_____

What is your experience like with other people who exhibit Three energy?

_____

_____

_____

_____

_____

_____

_____

_____

_____

_____

_____

_____

_____

_____

_____

_____

_____

_____

_____

_____

_____

_____

_____

Reflections on
BEING AN
ENNEAGRAM THREE

As you embark on this profound inner journey, it's essential to take a moment to revisit the very origin of your path. Within this section, we invite you to reflect upon the beginnings of your Enneagram journey and how it gently unfolded before you. Delving into past feelings and behaviors is a natural and important aspect of this process.

As a Three, your greatest strength is your unwavering inner drive to manifest your dreams and achieve success. The following prompts offer you a profound opportunity for self-reflection.

It's quite likely that you had specific reactions when you first discovered your dominant energy at Type Three. These reactions are all part of the ongoing journey as you gradually transition from mere reactions to intentional responses. It's essential to explore your feelings but not to become ensnared or overwhelmed by what you feel. Remember, feelings are transient in nature. As you navigate through your emotions, you'll discover immense fulfillment at the deeper layers of this exploration. Embrace your innate curiosity and approach this journey with the wonder of a beginner's mind as you unveil more and more about your authentic self and how you present yourself to the world. In connecting with the reality of your inner guidance and greatness, you may be pleasantly surprised by the fears that once held you back.

It's important to acknowledge that not every attribute, characteristic, or behavior associated with Type Three will necessarily resonate with your unique experience of this energy. This realization is a golden opportunity to unearth uncharted aspects of your being that have previously eluded your awareness. The process of discovering your authentic self is a profound journey that promises to broaden your mind, heal your heart, and rejuvenate your body in unprecedented ways. This deep dive will allow your spirit to fully embrace and embody your core values, in harmony with your natural gift of orchestrating success and bringing your aspirations to life. We wholeheartedly encourage you not to hold back but to embrace this journey as it carries you to uncharted territories within your own being, revealing facets of yourself you have yet to explore. This is our heartfelt wish for you.

Grounding Meditation

As I move into self-reflection and internal exploration,
I will meditate on each of these prompts and gently notice
what comes up for me as I breathe into stillness.

I am ready to begin with three cleansing breaths.

I am releasing any tension that I am holding on to with each exhale.

I am grounded and present to the sensations in my body.

I am open and aware of the feelings in my heart.

I am not attached to the thoughts that float by.

I am ready to explore what being a Three means to me.

I will embrace all aspects of my personality and gently
work toward becoming more accepting of myself.

My reactions when I discovered my dominant energy as a Type Three:

_____

_____

_____

_____

_____

_____

_____

_____

_____

_____

_____

_____

_____

_____

_____

_____

_____

_____

_____

_____

_____

My feelings about being a Three:

_____

_____

_____

_____

_____

_____

_____

_____

_____

_____

_____

_____

_____

_____

_____

_____

_____

_____

_____

_____

_____

_____

My hopes for discovering more about my Three energy:

_____
_____
_____
_____
_____
_____
_____
_____
_____
_____
_____
_____
_____
_____
_____
_____
_____
_____
_____
_____
_____
_____

My fears around seeing myself as I truly am:

_____

_____

_____

_____

_____

_____

_____

_____

_____

_____

_____

_____

_____

_____

_____

_____

_____

_____

_____

_____

_____

_____

Observations about myself that support Three as my dominant type:

Aspects and descriptors of Three energy that I do not feel connected with:

_____

_____

_____

_____

_____

_____

_____

_____

_____

_____

_____

Are these aspects I do not feel connected with indicators
of any personal challenges that I may overlook?

_____

_____

_____

_____

_____

_____

_____

_____

_____

_____

_____

What are my core values that align with my Three energy?

_____
_____
_____
_____
_____
_____
_____
_____
_____
_____
_____
_____
_____
_____
_____
_____
_____
_____
_____
_____
_____
_____

Reflections on my actions and beliefs around my core values:

Ways I have honored my core values recently:

_____

_____

_____

_____

_____

_____

_____

_____

_____

_____

_____

_____

_____

_____

_____

_____

_____

_____

_____

_____

_____

_____

_____

What do I wish people knew about me?

_____
_____
_____
_____
_____
_____
_____
_____
_____
_____
_____
_____
_____
_____
_____
_____
_____
_____
_____
_____
_____
_____
_____
_____
_____
_____

MY EARLY MESSAGES AND EXPERIENCES

As you embark on this journey, take a moment to reflect on the early messages and messengers that have shaped your path. You might discover that your childhood experiences, influenced by the dominant energy at Three, instilled a deep sense of achievement and success within you while simultaneously cementing your aversion to failure.

These early reactions and responses have left an indelible mark on your being. You absorbed messages, often subconsciously, which shaped your perspective and behavior. It's as if these messages were etched into your soul, inaccessible without the guiding light of deep inner work. As you navigated into adulthood, these feelings and beliefs traveled with you, influencing how you approached life. Over time, you may have cultivated an inner narrative that drove you to prove your worth and value, seeking love and validation. However, it's essential to acknowledge that this approach may have become a double-edged sword, posing certain challenges.

Looking back, you may start to notice aspects of your life that resonate strongly with the energy of Type Three. As you reflect on your life's unfolding, who or what stands out as a pivotal influence in your development? Comparing and contrasting your life experiences, the individuals who left lasting imprints, and the indelible impressions etched in your heart is an integral part of this introspective expedition.

As you begin to unearth these deep-seated experiences and emotions, embrace them with honesty and self-compassion. Allow yourself to honor and accept whatever feelings arise. Recall the joy and carefree spirit of your childhood when you delighted in life's simple pleasures just for the sake of enjoyment. Hold on to these memories as you continue your journey, for they are an integral part of the process that will lead you to rediscover your authentic self. Your past, like a treasure chest of genuine and important emotions and insights, has much to reveal. This is an invitation to explore with an open heart, for through the layers of your own history, you will find the radiant emergence of your authentic self.

Grounding Meditation

As I move into self-reflection and internal exploration,
I will meditate on these prompts and gently notice
what comes up as I breathe into stillness.

I am ready to begin with three cleansing breaths.

I am inhaling peace and exhaling tension.

I am ready to embark on a journey into my past.

I will honor my experience as I recall childhood memories.

My past does not define me.

I can explore what was, accept what is, and embrace what will be.

My most vivid memory of how my Three energy
showed up when I was a child:

_____

_____

_____

_____

_____

_____

_____

_____

_____

_____

_____

_____

_____

_____

_____

_____

_____

_____

_____

When I recall feeling valued and worthy, these are the
people and experiences that come to mind:

_____

_____

_____

_____

_____

_____

_____

_____

_____

_____

_____

_____

_____

_____

_____

_____

_____

_____

_____

_____

I can create space in my life for more of these positive influences by:

_____

_____

_____

_____

_____

_____

_____

_____

_____

_____

_____

_____

_____

_____

_____

_____

_____

_____

_____

_____

_____

_____

When I think back to my childhood, I remember being proud of:

_____

_____

_____

_____

_____

_____

_____

_____

_____

_____

_____

_____

_____

_____

_____

_____

_____

_____

_____

_____

_____

_____

_____

Activities I enjoyed as a child:

Reflections on how these activities
brought feelings of pure joy and happiness:

_____

_____

_____

_____

_____

_____

_____

_____

_____

_____

_____

_____

_____

_____

_____

_____

_____

_____

_____

_____

_____

_____

Happiness is part
of the flow of life.

If you remain rigid,
then happiness will
flow right past you.

Allow yourself
the gift of letting
go and ease into the
flow of whatever may
come your way.

I can cultivate small moments of happiness in my everyday life by:

Reflections on
MY PURPOSE AND
MY "PUZZLE PIECE"

Let's imagine the world as a puzzle, and envision each one of us holding a piece that, when placed, helps create a more complete and harmonious world. You possess a truly unique gift to offer to the world; imagine it as if you are the holder of a vital piece of a grand, intricate puzzle. Yet to truly offer this gift, we must be willing to embark on our own inner journey.

When we embrace this inner work, we gain the strength and clarity needed to step forward and make our unique contribution. This courageous act sets a beautiful chain reaction in motion, allowing others to find the inspiration and courage to contribute as well.

In the upcoming section, we extend a warm invitation to you, encouraging you to (re)awaken the passions and interests that stir deep within your soul, those beautiful aspects of yourself that you'd love to revive and share with the world. You might notice a strong emotional response to social injustices; this very reaction could be a hidden passion or a point of personal growth waiting to be unveiled. Your dedication to a particular societal issue could hold the key to discovering your unique place and voice in contributing to the collective healing of humanity. Perhaps your heart resonates deeply with environmental causes, or you're deeply affected by the suffering of animals. This is your precious opportunity to unearth and delve into what truly matters to you.

Consider what consistently draws your attention and captivates your mind—whether it's art, music, literature, social causes, theater, science, spirituality, parenting, or family. Why do these topics continue to surface for you? Use this opportunity to delve deeper into the aspects of your life where you find an abundance of energy or even areas that may initially appear exhausting. This is your chance to sculpt and refine your unique puzzle piece (and yes, we all have one or more) so that you can stand with gratitude and presence, fully aware of the significance of your contribution. As we awaken to our own purpose, we naturally have the capacity to awaken those around us, igniting a chain reaction of positive change.

Explore the boundless possibilities that lie ahead, and remember that your piece of the puzzle is invaluable to creating a world that's more complete, compassionate, and connected.

Grounding Meditation

As I move into self-reflection and internal exploration,
I will meditate on these prompts and gently notice
what comes up as I breathe into stillness.

I am ready to begin with three cleansing breaths.

I am releasing any tension that I am holding
in my body with each exhale.

I am inhaling into the wholeness of the Universe
and exhaling whatever may be troubling me.

I am open to exploring my place in the world.

I am willing to explore my purpose and (re)discover the
unique puzzle piece I hold to contribute to the world.

My life has meaning, and my presence matters.

I am accepting of whatever comes up for me at this moment.

What contributions do I want to make in this world?

_____

_____

_____

_____

_____

_____

_____

_____

_____

_____

_____

_____

_____

_____

_____

_____

_____

_____

_____

_____

_____

_____

Reflections on how I align my daily actions
with my deeper sense of achievement:

What inspires me?

_____
_____
_____
_____
_____
_____
_____
_____
_____
_____
_____
_____
_____
_____
_____
_____
_____
_____
_____
_____
_____
_____
_____

How have I limited myself in finding sources of inspiration? How can I open myself to new experiences? Have I considered engaging with new people, places, music, art, literature, and so on?

_____

_____

_____

_____

_____

_____

_____

_____

_____

_____

_____

_____

_____

_____

_____

_____

_____

_____

_____

_____

_____

_____

How is my success and focus on achievement affected by others?

_____

_____

_____

_____

_____

_____

_____

_____

_____

_____

_____

_____

_____

_____

_____

_____

_____

_____

_____

_____

_____

_____

_____

_____

What am I known for? How does this affect how I view myself?

The quality
of your life
will reflect
how deep you
are willing
to go to touch
your own soul.

What personal, professional, spiritual, and/or life
roles contribute to my sense of identity?

_____

_____

_____

_____

_____

_____

_____

_____

_____

_____

_____

_____

_____

_____

_____

_____

_____

_____

_____

_____

_____

_____

Can I allow myself to see my self-worth outside of external validation? What does that look like in real life?

I am very passionate about:

_____

_____

_____

_____

_____

_____

_____

_____

_____

_____

_____

_____

_____

_____

_____

_____

_____

_____

_____

_____

_____

_____

Reflections on my current projects, work, and endeavors:

How are these feeding my spirit or draining my energy?

HOW MY THREE
ENERGY SHOWS UP

Embarking on this transformative journey offers you a unique opportunity to explore your inner landscape as a Three. It's a path filled with intriguing paradoxes, where your innate drive for success and the pursuit of greatness often intersects with the need for external validation, potentially leading you away from your authentic self. This journey encourages you to navigate this paradox, seeking a healthier, more aligned energy and a deeper understanding of who you truly are.

At times, your definition of success and achievement may become clouded by external pressures, and the desire for validation can pull you in different directions. This might lead you to adopt characteristics and shortcuts that don't necessarily resonate with your authentic self. It's within this complexity that the inner work comes into play, guiding you to elevate your energy and reconnect with your authentic self.

When you release the burden of constantly striving to become the "best version of yourself," you are able to rediscover the person you were inherently meant to be. This reconnection to your authentic self is aligned to connecting with spirit, where honesty, self-acceptance, and a kind, generous energy flourish from within. You no longer feel compelled to hide behind a facade but instead open yourself to the world, revealing the incredible and authentic you.

Your natural charisma and inner drive are precious gifts you have to share with the world. As you broaden your focus beyond personal gain, you'll discover that your real potential lies in uplifting those around you. When you allow yourself to extend beyond the boundaries of "me and mine," the possibilities for meaningful success and genuine greatness expand exponentially. This journey is an invitation to look within and identify any self-imposed limitations that might be hindering you from fully stepping into the astonishing person you were created to be.

Embrace this process with an open heart and a curious spirit. Through introspection and self-discovery, you'll find that you possess an abundant capacity for growth, authenticity, and an impact that can reach far beyond your personal aspirations. As you explore your journey as a Three, remember that the authentic you radiates truthfulness, love, and light to the world.

Grounding Meditation

As I move into self-reflection and internal exploration,
I will meditate on these prompts and gently notice
what comes up as I breathe into stillness.

I am ready to begin with three cleansing breaths.

I am inhaling into presence and exhaling negativity and judgment.

I am ready to explore my Threeness.

I will allow myself to reflect on how I show up to myself and others.

I will acknowledge any judgment or criticism that
arises with Grace and compassion for myself.

I will embrace all parts of my being as valid and valuable.

Reflect back on the "Levels of Development" section (page 14) for this exercise.

I was aware of the high side of my Three energy this week when:

_____

_____

_____

_____

_____

_____

_____

_____

_____

_____

_____

_____

_____

_____

_____

_____

_____

_____

_____

_____

Reflect back on the "Levels of Development" section (page 14) for this exercise.

I was aware of the low side of my Three energy this week when:

_____

_____

_____

_____

_____

_____

_____

_____

_____

_____

_____

_____

_____

_____

_____

_____

_____

_____

_____

_____

_____

Always examine what "the best" means to you and what you are willing to relinquish to constantly chase this elusive status.

My reflections on what being the best means to me:

_____

_____

_____

_____

_____

_____

_____

_____

_____

_____

_____

_____

_____

_____

_____

_____

_____

_____

_____

_____

_____

_____

My reactions to failure:

_____
_____
_____
_____
_____
_____
_____
_____
_____
_____
_____
_____
_____
_____
_____
_____
_____
_____
_____
_____
_____
_____
_____

Ways that I experience challenges to who I think
I am and how I show up in the world:

_____
_____
_____
_____
_____
_____
_____
_____
_____
_____
_____
_____
_____
_____
_____
_____
_____
_____
_____
_____
_____

What parts of myself do I hide from others and why?

How do I express love and affection?

When do I feel valuable, worthy, or successful?

Who am I outside of my accomplishments? What makes me proud?

_____

_____

_____

_____

_____

_____

_____

_____

_____

_____

_____

_____

_____

_____

_____

_____

_____

_____

_____

_____

_____

You must embrace
your own being
and accept yourself
exactly as you are.
This is a first
step in belonging.
Never let anyone
determine whether
or not you belong.

That choice is yours.

What does belonging mean to me? How have I sought
out belonging and connection in my life?

_____

_____

_____

_____

_____

_____

_____

_____

_____

_____

_____

_____

_____

_____

_____

_____

_____

_____

_____

_____

_____

What do other people do for me that makes me feel seen?

How do I make others feel seen?

How do other people describe me?

Fill the page with words, phrases, and drawings.
Allow for the flow of creativity and freedom.

How do I describe myself?

Fill the page with words, phrases, and drawings.
Allow for the flow of creativity and freedom.

Reflections on
IMPOSTOR SYNDROME AND FINDING MY IDENTITY

Along your journey, it is important to honor the different aspects of your identity as a Three. In this section you're invited to explore the intricate balance between your outward appearance as a superhuman capable of achieving remarkable feats and the hidden internal struggle that occasionally simmers beneath the surface. This juxtaposition is where truthfulness unfolds, fostering a genuine connection with your authentic self.

You may be well-acquainted with the phenomenon known as impostor syndrome, which can stir up powerful emotions, including a fear of failure. This fear may be linked closely to your personal value, self-worth, and identity, sometimes leading you into uncertain waters. To navigate these depths and discover your authentic self, it's essential to embark on the inner work that will guide you toward your releasing what no longer serves you.

Feelings of not being enough or the fear of being seen as worthless can be daunting companions. They can drive you to seek sources for external validation and acknowledgment, often at the expense of your genuine emotions, beliefs, and desires. This may compel you to maintain the appearance of success, projecting an impressive exterior to the world. However, beneath the polished surface, you may sometimes feel like you're teetering on the precipice, questioning whether you are indeed as great as you appear. The nagging worry that someone might eventually see through your seemingly flawless exterior and unveil an impostor who feels hollow and undeserving can be challenging to bear.

Your journey calls for a courageous confrontation of this fear and a confident step into your authentic self. Recognize that you do not need to be what others expect of you, and that honoring your genuine self is an act of Grace. As you walk this path, you are invited to acknowledge that true greatness lies in embracing your unique gifts and sharing your authentic self with the world.

In this section, you are encouraged to delve into your experiences with impostor syndrome and the complex intricacies of identity projection. This may be a tender and vulnerable exploration for you, but remember that compassion for yourself is a powerful ally as you allow these emotions to surface. Embrace the authenticity of your emotions and resist the urge to sidestep honest expression. Stay present with the profound truthfulness that resides within you as a Three. By doing so, you'll discover the depth of your inner strength and the richness of your unique journey toward authenticity.

Grounding Meditation

As I move into self-reflection and internal exploration,
I will meditate on these prompts and gently notice
what comes up as I breathe into stillness.

I am ready to begin with three cleansing breaths.

I am inhaling into patience and love and
exhaling self-doubt and criticism.

I will remain in presence and choose a path
of empathy and compassion.

I will be honest with myself.

I can look at everything that makes me who I am
while remaining present and understanding.

I am valuable and worthy just as I am.

What does success look like for me as a Three?

What does failure look like for me as a Three?

How do I experience impostor syndrome? What
does it look like and what does it feel like?

What/who makes me feel worthy and valued?

How does my self-worth fluctuate? What does it look like?

How does this affect how I view and treat others?

I am proficient in:

_____

_____

_____

_____

_____

_____

_____

_____

_____

_____

_____

_____

_____

_____

_____

_____

_____

_____

_____

_____

_____

How do I shape shift or manipulate my actions and behaviors to fill a role? What does it actually look like in real life?

What steps can I take to pause and change my course of action when I notice my self-worth feels dependent on external validation?

_____

_____

_____

_____

_____

_____

_____

_____

_____

_____

_____

_____

_____

_____

_____

_____

_____

_____

_____

_____

_____

How can I use my ambition to motivate and advocate for others?

Unleash the potential that is in another and you unleash the potential that is in you.

MATSHONA DHLIWAYO

We are surrounded
by Grace in every
moment of our lives.
Grace always comes
through when we allow
ourselves to embrace
and experience the
warmth of its existence.
Let love and light in.

Allow Grace to
lead your actions today.

What does Grace look like for me as a Three?

Reflections on
MY RELATIONSHIP
TO SHAME AND GUILT

As a Three, you may experience a wall of shame surrounding a particular unhealed or unexplored internal wound, often tied to how you perceive your presence in the world. This invisible "wall" forms a barrier that keeps you from accessing your authentic self. How this barrier is addressed or ignored varies from person to person. For some, this shame could trace back to early memories of feeling unwanted, unworthy, unseen, or not good enough. Each individual navigates their shame in their own way, but when we find ourselves entangled in toxic patterns of behavior, this internal shame often morphs into an outward expression, directing our emotions toward others in one form or another. At first glance, it may seem unexpected for shame and guilt to be at the center of Type Three. However, both emotions, while expressed differently, often share roots in a deeply ingrained need to prove one's worth.

As a Three, it's probable that something in your early life sparked a need to establish your worth based on your achievements rather than your intrinsic value as a person. In this process of self-preservation, you might have built a protective wall around your heart to shield yourself from feelings of being unworthy of love just for being you. It's possible that, either directly or indirectly, you've learned that love is earned through accomplishments and excellence. For some, this can lead to a belief that unveiling their authentic selves would expose them to the ridicule of being seen as an impostor, a fraud, or someone undeserving of love and attention. These are the false narratives that can linger within you for a long time. The inner work process you embark upon will enable you to identify and remove these false narratives, marking a vital step in your journey toward becoming your authentic self. As you relinquish the false self you've crafted, you'll rewire the connection between your head and your heart.

Now, with your heart fully awakened, the walls you've constructed to keep shame at bay no longer serve any purpose. This newfound realization allows you to step into your full potential, becoming a person who allows their innate gifts to flow freely and authentically.

In this section, you're invited to gently explore the roots of your shame and guilt, paving the way to cultivate self-love and acceptance. These exercises are thoughtfully designed to assist you in moving through the challenges of your energy, guiding you on a path to reconnect with all the goodness, love, and light that reside within you. Grant yourself the space to be truthful in your experiences and resist the temptation to distort your reactions to what surfaces. This is a gentle journey toward healing and self-discovery.

Grounding Meditation

As I move into self-reflection and internal exploration,
I will meditate on these prompts and gently notice
what comes up as I breathe into stillness.

I am ready to begin with three cleansing breaths.

I am inhaling a sense of calm and peace
and exhaling tension and worry.

I acknowledge my shame and guilt, and I am willing
to gently explore what's underneath.

I will explore my relationship to my shame
and guilt with intentional presence.

I accept shame and guilt as natural human emotions, and
I acknowledge that they do not define who I am.

I will accept my shame and guilt as an internal warning system
to seek out opportunities for growth and self-reflection.

How do I define my shame and guilt? How are they different?

What/who makes me experience feelings of shame and/or guilt?

_____

_____

_____

_____

_____

_____

_____

_____

_____

_____

_____

_____

_____

_____

_____

_____

_____

_____

_____

_____

Guilt is not a response to anger; it is a response to one's own actions or lack of action. If it leads to change, then it can be useful since it is then no longer guilt but the beginning of knowledge.

AUDRE LORDE

Your greatest achievement will always be how well you give and receive love.

Can I explore the roots of my shame and challenge
them in a healthy and productive way?

_____

_____

_____

_____

_____

_____

_____

_____

_____

_____

_____

_____

_____

_____

_____

_____

_____

_____

_____

_____

_____

How do I channel or redirect my shame and guilt?
What does that actually look like?

_____

_____

_____

_____

_____

_____

_____

_____

_____

_____

_____

_____

_____

_____

_____

_____

_____

_____

_____

When am I deceitful, and what does it look like?

What does it look like when I need a break? Do I know how to rest? What gets in the way of my ability to pause and allow myself a respite from the constant forward motion?

_____
_____
_____
_____
_____
_____
_____
_____
_____
_____
_____
_____
_____
_____
_____
_____
_____
_____
_____

Who am I outside of what I do? Can I describe myself without using my achievements or accomplishments as self-identifiers?

_____

_____

_____

_____

_____

_____

_____

_____

_____

_____

_____

_____

_____

_____

_____

_____

_____

_____

_____

_____

_____

_____

_____

What am I ashamed of and why?

What am I truly proud of and why?

Reflections on
MY VIRTUE OF TRUTHFULNESS

Within the realm of the Enneagram, the virtue for Type Three is truthfulness. Embracing this virtue becomes an inviting concept when you consider it as the free-flowing energy that allows you to acknowledge, appreciate and fully honor your authentic self. It's the understanding that you don't need to prove anything to be worthy of love; you are inherently deserving of it. As someone who resonates with Type Three, truthfulness manifests when you embark on the inner work journey and access the gifts found on the high side of Three.

On your path toward this virtue, you might encounter some familiar roadblocks, especially the alluring temptation—or fixation as it is known in the Enneagram—of vanity that can ensnare a Type Three. You've always set your sights high, and the mere thought of stumbling or faltering is something you simply don't entertain in your world. While facing challenges, there might be moments when you're tempted to take shortcuts or stretch the truth a bit to maintain your place at the pinnacle and satisfy your deep craving for recognition and validation. Your unwavering aversion to anything resembling failure influences the way you perceive yourself, anchoring your self-image and self-worth to your impressive accomplishments. Remember, in this space of self-reflection and intentional compassion, you can begin to acknowledge these feelings and work toward a more balanced approach on your journey to personal growth and fulfillment.

In this exploration, it is important to understand that your true power and your authentic self can reemerge when you embrace the gift of truthfulness as a Three. You can step into a healthy space where the need for stillness and emotional honesty allows you to move away from the burdens of shame, deceit, and vanity. These are false emotions that have been obscuring your true heart. By choosing to enter the transformative space of self-awareness, you'll access authenticity and truthfulness. Here, you can rediscover your balance, your connection to Grace, and the inner courage to be your authentic self.

Exploring your connection to the virtue of truthfulness is another significant step on your journey toward unearthing your authentic self. It's an invitation to self-discovery, a path that can lead you to wholeness, clarity, and a deeper sense of who you are.

Grounding Meditation

As I move into self-reflection and internal exploration,
I will meditate on these prompts and gently notice
what comes up as I breathe into stillness.

I am ready to begin with three cleansing breaths.

I am inhaling into truthfulness and exhaling any
tension or hesitation that comes up for me.

As I explore truthfulness, I seek out opportunities
to allow it to flow naturally.

Truthfulness is my access to Grace.

Truthfulness is always present within me.

I allow myself to embrace the gift of truthfulness
by releasing what no longer serves me.

How has truthfulness manifested in my life, and what did it bring?

_____

_____

_____

_____

_____

_____

_____

_____

_____

_____

_____

_____

_____

_____

_____

_____

_____

_____

_____

_____

_____

How has truthfulness eluded me?
What comes up for me by asking this question?

Truthfulness allows our moral compass to show us the way forward when tempted by deceit.

What am I willing to surrender to embrace truthfulness?

When do I notice my tendency toward vanity and deceit fading and my ability to access the virtue of truthfulness developing?

_____

_____

_____

_____

_____

_____

_____

_____

_____

_____

_____

_____

_____

_____

_____

_____

_____

_____

_____

_____

Reflecting on how I define my identity and self-worth, my experience with impostor syndrome, and my relationship to shame and guilt, can I explore what my path to the embodiment of truthfulness looks like?

_____

_____

_____

_____

_____

_____

_____

_____

_____

_____

_____

_____

_____

_____

_____

_____

_____

_____

_____

_____

_____

_____

What are a few small actions I can take right now to bring myself into the present moment, such as taking a deep breath, stretching, going for a run, or savoring a sip of tea or coffee?

What are a few mantras I will use daily to bring myself back to the present and move into a space where I can access the virtue of truthfulness?

Example: I will allow myself to step back and let who I truly am shine without feeling the need to perform.

_____

_____

_____

_____

_____

_____

_____

_____

_____

_____

_____

_____

_____

_____

_____

_____

_____

Discovering Connections to
OTHER ENNEAGRAM ENERGIES

Consider the Enneagram energies as nine individual gifts, each uniquely enriching the tapestry of your being. Within each of us, these nine energies coexist, and far too often, our fixation on our Enneagram type limits our perspective, hindering exploration of the eight other invaluable energies residing within us. It's vital to recognize that every human being requires the presence of these nine energies to achieve wholeness and completeness.

At each point of the Enneagram, a precious gift awaits, illuminating the path of self-discovery. At point One the gift is integrity, a beacon that guides you with a resolute moral compass. Point Two bestows the gift of pure love, fostering a spirit of generosity and an open heart for giving and receiving. Point Three endows you with the drive to accomplish and achieve great things, not just for personal gain but for the greater good of all. Point Four graces you with the capacity to embrace the world's beauty, holding it through love, empathy, and profound compassion while connecting deeply with human emotions. Point Five gifts you with the power of observation and the ability to discern solutions that might otherwise go unnoticed. At point Six you receive the gift of resilience, enabling you to cultivate the awareness of what is needed to keep us all protected, prepared, and unwavering in the face of adversity. Point Seven brings the gift of optimism, positivity, and spontaneity, infusing even the most challenging tasks with the spirit of joyfulness. Point Eight's gift is leadership, guiding us forward with the purity and strength of an innocent heart, always mindful of keeping our collective well-being intact. Finally, at point Nine, you are blessed with the gift of pure peace, a peace that transcends understanding and can only arise from a heart transformed by light and love.

Imagine that someone has lovingly gifted you with these nine beautifully wrapped presents. Why would you choose to open only one?

In this section, you are encouraged to embark on a journey through all nine Enneagram energies, to explore the connections to your wings, lines, and arrows, as well as the points that may not be part of your primary access. It's important to remember that you always have access to all nine energies, and sometimes, it takes a more deliberate effort to unearth these connections. Embrace this exploration with an open heart, for it's a step toward a deeper understanding of your authentic, multifaceted self, filled with infinite possibilities.

Grounding Meditation

As I move into self-reflection and internal exploration,
I will meditate on these prompts and gently notice
what comes up as I breathe into stillness.

I am ready to begin with three cleansing breaths.

I am inhaling into expansiveness and exhaling constriction.

I have the gift of all nine Enneagram energies within me.

I can freely explore my energy at all nine points.

I am not limited by my type.

I acknowledge my energy and connection to point Nine and
point Six and utilize them for growth and awareness.

I can freely access my wings at point Two and point Four.

THE BODY CENTER: 8-9-1

In the Body Center, we gain access to our body's wisdom and gut intuition. The Body Center energy is focused on action—affecting the world or environment to avoid being influenced, controlled, or limited by it, and expressing anger or rage in different ways.

What does it look like for me to access
the energies within the Body Center?

Eight

_____
_____
_____
_____
_____

Nine

_____
_____
_____
_____
_____

One

_____
_____
_____
_____
_____

THE HEART CENTER: 2-3-4

In the Heart Center, we gain access to our capacity for emotional honesty and human connection. The Heart Center energy is focused on emotions, self-image, and value—determining your identity and the value you place on your identity plays a key role in how you access the Heart Center energy.

What does it look like for me to access the
energies within the Heart Center?

Two

_____
_____
_____
_____
_____

Three

_____
_____
_____
_____

Four

_____
_____
_____
_____
_____

THE HEAD CENTER: 5-6-7

In the Head Center, we gain access to our ability to reflect, process, and internalize information. The wisdom we have access to in the Head Center energies allows us to cultivate the space we need for objectivity and inner guidance.

What does it look like for me to access the
energies within the Head Center?

Five

_____

_____

_____

_____

_____

Six

_____

_____

_____

_____

_____

Seven

_____

_____

_____

_____

_____

Do I face any challenges connecting to particular
Enneagram energies? Can I explore this further?

_____

_____

_____

_____

_____

_____

_____

_____

_____

_____

_____

_____

_____

_____

_____

_____

_____

_____

_____

_____

_____

Reflecting on the connection to my Two wing, how can Two energy bring me compassion and empathy for others while enabling my natural gifts to be shared with those around me?

_____
_____
_____
_____
_____
_____
_____
_____
_____
_____
_____
_____
_____
_____
_____
_____
_____
_____
_____
_____
_____

Self-love is an ocean and your heart is a vessel. Make it full, and any excess will spill over into the lives of the people you hold dear. But you must come first.

BEAU TAPLIN

Reflecting on the connection to my Four wing, how can Four energy bring me the emotional awareness I need to deal with how I feel and honor these emotions as valid and important?

_____

_____

_____

_____

_____

_____

_____

_____

_____

_____

_____

_____

_____

_____

_____

_____

_____

_____

_____

_____

_____

_____

The whole point of being alive is to evolve into the complete person you were intended to be.

OPRAH WINFREY

At point Three, I share a connection to point Nine, which provides an opportunity to explore the gifts and challenges of this energy. On the upside, this grounding energy can help me slow down and find the space to collaborate, harmonize, and connect with others. On the downside, this energy can foster apathy and aimlessness. How have I experienced Nine energy in my life?

_Relaxation is the prerequisite for that inner
expansion that allows a person to express
the source of inspiration and joy within._

DEEPAK CHOPRA

What does it look like when I tap into the inner peace, tranquility, and stillness at point Nine? How does my connection to point Nine affect my actions, behaviors, and beliefs?

Care for your psyche . . . know thyself, for once we know ourselves, we may learn how to care for ourselves.

SOCRATES

At point Three, I share a connection to point Six, which provides an opportunity to explore the gifts and challenges of this energy. On the upside, this energy can allow for a clear focus and collaborative spirit to flourish while helping me stay accountable. On the downside, this energy can make me distrustful of others, scattered, and highly indecisive. How have I experienced Six energy in my life?

_____

_____

_____

_____

_____

_____

_____

_____

_____

_____

_____

_____

_____

_____

_____

_____

_____

_____

_____

When we tackle obstacles, we find hidden reserves of courage and resilience we did not know we had. And it is only when we are faced with failure do we realize that these resources were always there within us. We only need to find them and move on with our lives.

A. P. J. ABDUL KALAM

What does it look like when I am able to channel the truthfulness and problem-solving energy at point Six? How does my connection to point Six affect my actions, behaviors, and beliefs?

_____

_____

_____

_____

_____

_____

_____

_____

_____

_____

_____

_____

_____

_____

_____

_____

_____

_____

_____

_____

_____

Only those who dare to fail greatly.

can ever achieve greatly.

ROBERT F. KENNEDY

Resources for
CONTINUED EXPLORATION

If you would like to continue your Enneagram journey,
we invite you to visit our resources hub at:

DEBORAHEGERTON.COM/RESOURCES

and explore all of the resources we have gathered for you.
This resource hub is updated frequently, so make sure you
check back when you feel the need for a little inspiration.

You are also encouraged to read my books:

*Know Justice Know Peace: A Transformative Journey of Social Justice,
Anti-Racism, and Healing through the Power of the Enneagram*

*Enneagram Made Easy: Explore the Nine Personality Types of the
Enneagram to Open Your Heart, Find Joy, and Discover Your True Self*

**For easy access to the resources hub, use
your smartphone to scan this QR code:**

ABOUT THE AUTHOR

Deborah Threadgill Egerton, Ph.D., is an internationally respected psychotherapist, best-selling author, certified Enneagram teacher, unity and belonging advocate for the healing of humanity, consultant, coach, and spiritual teacher. Dr. Egerton specializes in working with the Enneagram to facilitate intentional change in individuals and organizations.

Affectionately referred to as "Dr. E," she has attained IEA Certification with Distinction for her groundbreaking utilization of the Enneagram in the realm of humanitarian healing. Her work is dedicated to dismantling marginalization and transcending the divisive practice of "othering," offering a guiding path toward the harmonious unification of our global community through the transformative forces of kindness and compassion. Dr. E serves as the president of the International Enneagram Association, the global entity responsible for educating, certifying, and accrediting practitioners, teachers, and schools. In her tenure with the IEA, she has been instrumental in fostering an environment of greater inclusivity and accessibility within the global Enneagram community. Her unwavering commitment to justice, equity, diversity, and inclusion has earned her the affectionate title of "Enneagram JEDI" among her peers.

Dr. E extends her coaching and mentoring expertise to a diverse spectrum of individuals, including best-selling authors, top-tier executives, spiritual luminaries, accomplished therapists, and a myriad of coaches, each hailing from distinct and varied backgrounds. For more than two decades, her work has focused on guiding humanity toward a deeper and more compassionate approach to inner work by harnessing the insights of the Enneagram. Her innovative approach to using the Enneagram in social justice and anti-racism work created a blueprint to reconnect people across all dimensions of diversity and has been implemented in various organizations and entities across the globe. She focuses her work on individuals and organizations to help them release false historical narratives and open their minds and hearts to a more compassionate and connected approach to life.

We hope you enjoyed this Hay House book. If you'd like to receive our online catalog featuring additional information on Hay House books and products, or if you'd like to find out more about the Hay Foundation, please contact:

HAY
HOUSE

Hay House LLC, P.O. Box 5100, Carlsbad, CA 92018-5100
(760) 431-7695 or (800) 654-5126
(760) 431-6948 (fax) or (800) 650-5115 (fax)
www.hayhouse.com® • www.hayfoundation.org

———

Published in Australia by: Hay House Australia Pty. Ltd.,
18/36 Ralph St., Alexandria NSW 2015
Phone: 612-9669-4299 • *Fax:* 612-9669-4144
www.hayhouse.com.au

Published in the United Kingdom by: Hay House UK, Ltd.,
The Sixth Floor, Watson House, 54 Baker Street, London W1U 7BU
Phone: +44 (0)20 3927 7290 • *Fax:* +44 (0)20 3927 7291
www.hayhouse.co.uk

Published in India by: Hay House Publishers India,
Muskaan Complex, Plot No. 3, B-2, Vasant Kunj, New Delhi 110 070
Phone: 91-11-4176-1620 • *Fax:* 91-11-4176-1630
www.hayhouse.co.in

———

Access New Knowledge.
Anytime. Anywhere.

Learn and evolve at your own pace
with the world's leading experts.

www.hayhouseU.com